Festive Christm

Colouring Book

De-ann Black

Published by Toffee Apple Publishing 2015

Colouring books by De-ann Black: Flower Hunter, Sea Dream, Bee Garden, Flower Bee, Autumn Garden, Summer Garden, Christmas Garden and Festive Christmas Colouring Book.

Fiction books by De-ann Black (Romance, Crime/Thrillers, Children's books). See her Amazon Author page or website for the full list of her books. Further details about De-ann's art, illustrations, fabric designs and books are available from her website. www.De-annBlack.com

Romance:

The Beemaster's Cottage
The Sewing Bee By The Sea
The Flower Hunter's Cottage
The Christmas Knitting Bee
The Sewing Bee & Afternoon Tea
The Tea Shop
The Vintage Sewing & Knitting Bee
Shed In The City
The Bakery By The Seaside
Champagne Chic Lemonade Money
Christmas Romance In Paris
The Chocolate Cake Shop In New York At Christmas
The Christmas Chocolatier
The Christmas Tea Shop & Bakery
Christmas Romance In Scotland
The Vintage Tea Dress Shop In Summer
The Fairytale Tea Dress Shop In Edinburgh
Dublin Girl - Hot Summer In The City
Oops! I'm The Paparazzi
The Cure For Love
The Tea Dress Shop At Christmas

Crime/Thrillers:

Electric Shadows
The Strife Of Riley
Shadows Of Murder

Children's books:

Faeriefied
Secondhand Spooks
Poison-Wynd
Science Fashion
School For Aliens
Wormhole Wynd

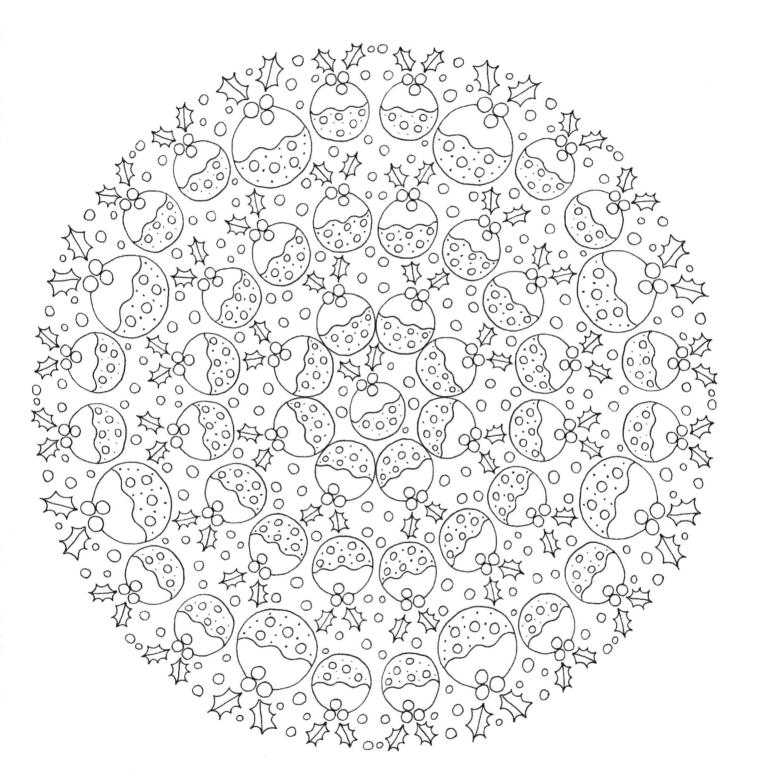

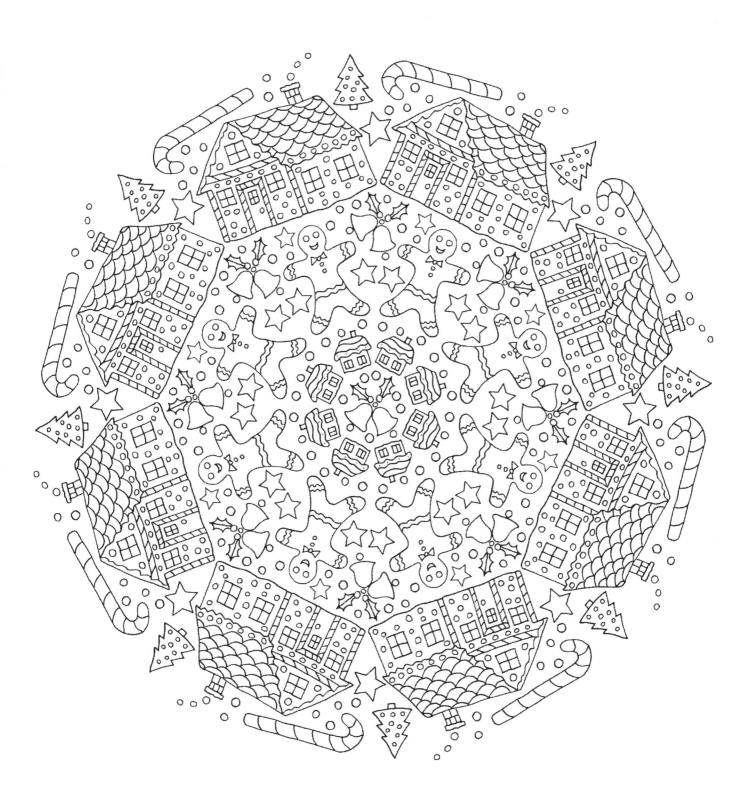

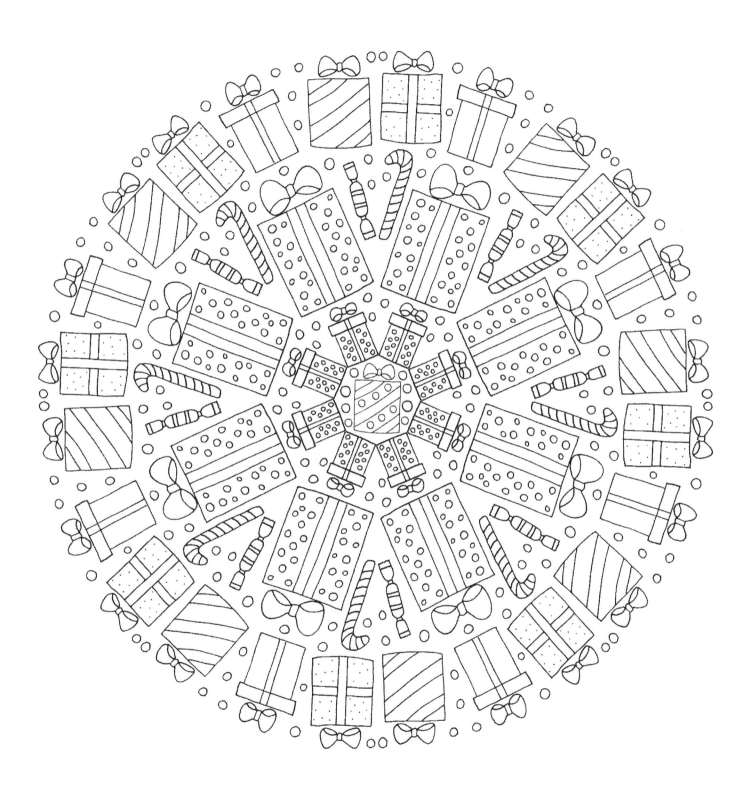

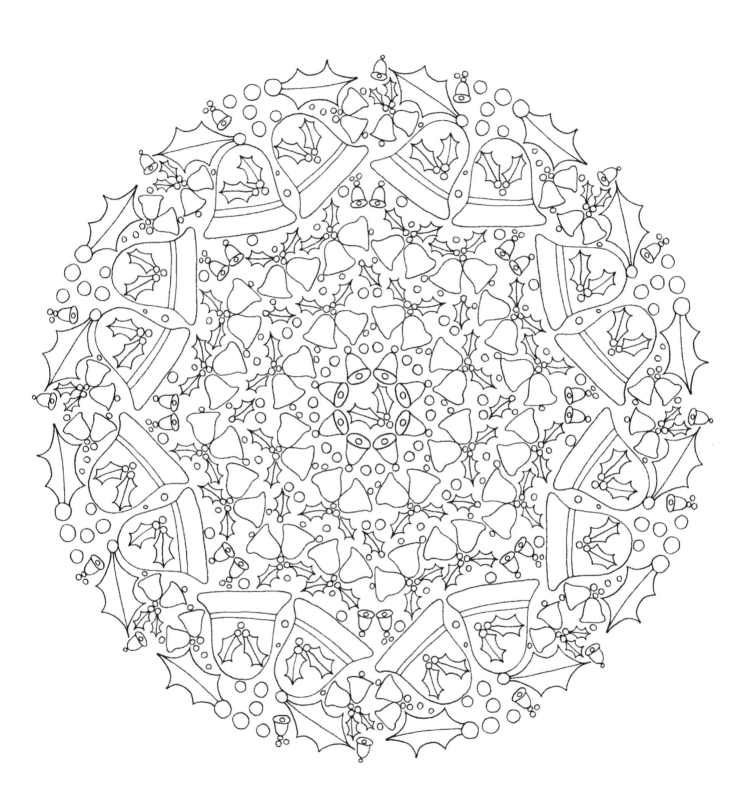

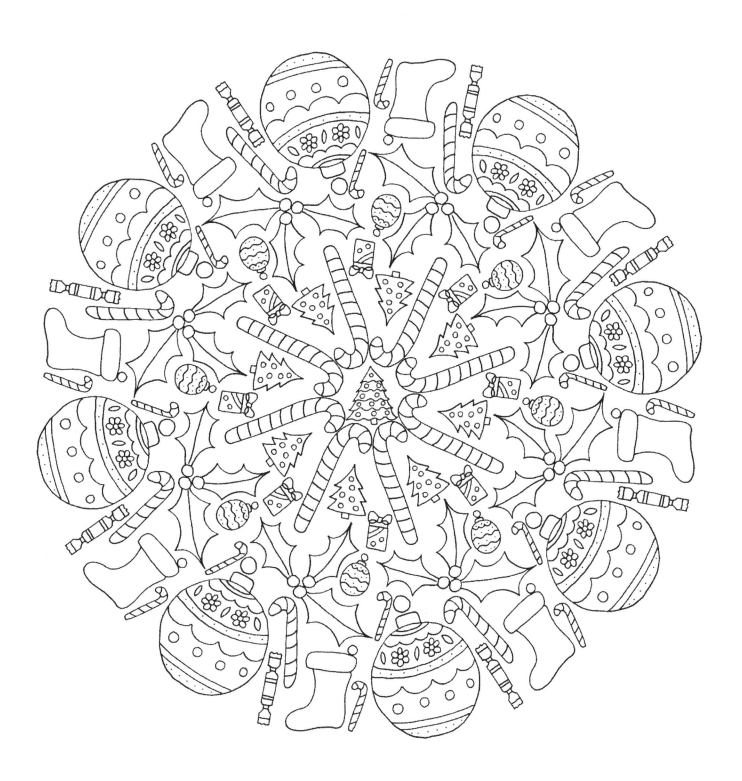

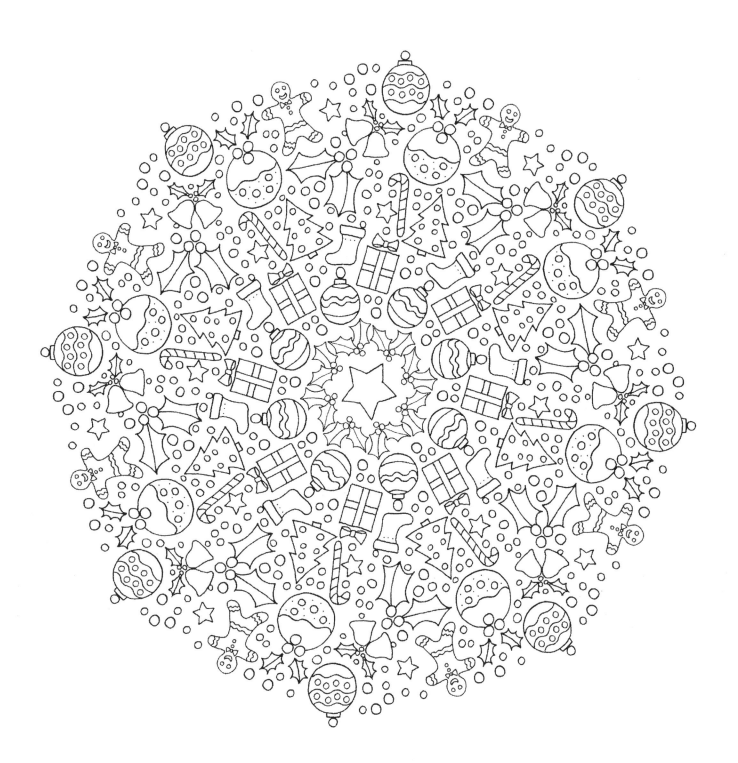